CU00821281

THE ROYAL HORTICULTURAL SOCIETY
FRUIT & VEG NOTEBOOK

Illustrations from the Royal Horticultural Society's Lindley Library

F
FRANCES LINCOLN LIMITED
PUBLISHERS

Frances Lincoln Limited
4 Torriano Mews
Torriano Avenue
London NW5 2RZ
www.franceslincoln.com

The Royal Horticultural Society
Fruit & Veg Notebook
Copyright © Frances Lincoln Limited 2007

Text and illustrations copyright © the Royal
Horticultural Society 2007
and printed under licence granted by the
Royal Horticultural Society, Registered
Charity number 222879. Profits from the sale
of this book are an important contribution to
the funds raised by the Royal Horticultural
Society. For more information visit our
website or call 0845 130 4646.

Website: www.rhs.org.uk

British Library cataloguing-in-publication data
A catalogue record for this book is available
from the British Library

Printed in China
ISBN 978-0-7112-2793-4
First Frances Lincoln edition 2007

A GROWING SOCIETY

Throughout its history, the Royal Horticultural Society has inspired people to discover new and interesting plants and encouraged an interest in gardening. This *RHS Fruit & Veg Notebook* is designed to help you to keep notes on your own discoveries.

With its spectacular flower shows, world-class gardens and the highest standards in advice, science and education, the RHS is at the heart of gardening today. To become a member, all you need is an interest in gardening. One of the many benefits of membership is free access to our Garden Advice Service covering such queries as where to buy and how to grow plants, plus advice on pests and diseases, identifying plants and garden products.

For more information please call our membership hotline on 0845 130 4646 or log onto our website: www.rhs.org.uk.

Front Cover: Hand-coloured engraving after Augusta Innes Withers, of the 'Hawthornden' apple, John Lindley's *Pomological Magazine,* Volume 1 (1827–28).
Back Cover: Chromolithograph by G. Severeyns of sixteen varieties of radishes, from the *Album Benary* (1876–82) by the Erfurt seedsman Ernst Benary.
Title Page: Colour-printed engraving by Pierre-Joseph Redouté, of redcurrants, from his *Choix des Plus Belles Fleurs* (1827–33).

CONTENTS

FRUIT

1. Frogmore Prolific

2. Small's Admirable.

3. Grenadier.

4. Golden Spire.

5. Sugarloaf Pippin.

6. Ringer.

7. Lord Derby

8. Bramley's Seedling

Chromolithograph by G. Severeyns after Edith E. Bull, of the apple 'Bramley's Seedling', from the *Herefordshire Pomona* by H. G. Bull and R. Hogg (1878–85).

APPLES

NAME/VARIETY/SUPPLIER	PLANTING & CULTIVATION NOTES

PRUNING NOTES	HARVEST DUE/ACTUAL DATE/YIELD

NAME/VARIETY/ SUPPLIER	PLANTING & CULTIVATION NOTES

PRUNING NOTES	HARVEST DUE/ACTUAL DATE/YIELD

Chromolithograph by G. Severeyns after Alice B. Ellis and Edith E. Bull, of the pear 'Duchesse d'Orléans', from the *Herefordshire Pomona* by H. G. Bull and R. Hogg (1878–85).

PEARS

NAME/VARIETY/ SUPPLIER	PLANTING & CULTIVATION NOTES

NAME/VARIETY/ SUPPLIER	PLANTING & CULTIVATION NOTES

PRUNING NOTES	HARVEST DUE/ACTUAL DATE/YIELD

Hand-coloured engraving after Augusta I. Withers, of the 'Mimms' plum, from John·Lindley's *Pomological Magazine*, Volume 1 (1827–28).

STONE FRUITS

NAME/VARIETY/ SUPPLIER	PLANTING & CULTIVATION NOTES

NAME/VARIETY/ SUPPLIER	PLANTING & CULTIVATION NOTES

PRUNING NOTES	HARVEST DUE/ACTUAL DATE/YIELD

NAME/VARIETY/ SUPPLIER	PLANTING & CULTIVATION NOTES

Hand-coloured engraving after Augusta I. Withers, of the 'Barnet' raspberry, from John Lindley's *Pomological Magazine,* Volume 1 (1827–28).

BERRIES

NAME/VARIETY/SUPPLIER	PLANTING & CULTIVATION NOTES

NAME/VARIETY/SUPPLIER	PLANTING & CULTIVATION NOTES

PRUNING NOTES	HARVEST DUE/ACTUAL DATE/YIELD

NAME/VARIETY/ SUPPLIER	PLANTING & CULTIVATION NOTES

NAME/VARIETY/ SUPPLIER	PLANTING & CULTIVATION NOTES

PRUNING NOTES	HARVEST DUE/ACTUAL DATE/YIELD

Hand-coloured engraving after Augusta I. Withers, of the 'Cambridge Botanic Garden' grape, from John Lindley's *Pomological Magazine*, Volume 1 (1827–28).

VINES

NAME/VARIETY/ SUPPLIER	PLANTING & CULTIVATION NOTES

NAME/VARIETY/ SUPPLIER	PLANTING & CULTIVATION NOTES

PRUNING NOTES	HARVEST DUE/ACTUAL DATE/YIELD

Chromolithograph by G. Severeyns of seven varieties of melons, from the *Album Benary* (1876–82) by the Erfurt seedsman Ernst Benary.

SPECIAL
INTEREST

NAME/VARIETY/ SUPPLIER	PLANTING & CULTIVATION NOTES

NAME/VARIETY/ SUPPLIER	PLANTING & CULTIVATION NOTES

PRUNING NOTES	HARVEST DUE/ACTUAL DATE/YIELD	

NAME/VARIETY/ SUPPLIER	PLANTING & CULTIVATION NOTES

NAME/VARIETY/SUPPLIER	PLANTING & CULTIVATION NOTES

PRUNING NOTES	HARVEST DUE/ACTUAL DATE/YIELD

VEGETABLES

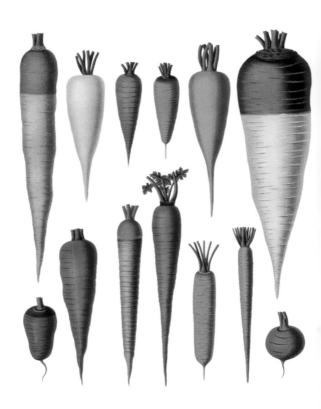

Chromolithograph by G. Severeyns of thirteen varieties of carrots, from the
Album Benary (1876–82) by the Erfurt seedsman Ernst Benary.

ROOTS
& TUBERS

NAME/VARIETY/ SUPPLIER	DATE SOWN & PROPAGATION NOTES

NAME/VARIETY/ SUPPLIER	DATE SOWN & PROPAGATION NOTES

PLANTING & CULTIVATION NOTES	HARVEST DUE/ACTUAL DATE/YIELD	

NAME/VARIETY/ SUPPLIER	DATE SOWN & PROPAGATION NOTES

Chromolithograph by G. Severeyns of six varieties of lettuces, from the *Album Benary* (1876–82) by the Erfurt seedsman Ernst Benary.

SALADS
& HERBS

NAME/VARIETY/ SUPPLIER	DATE SOWN & PROPAGATION NOTES

PLANTING & CULTIVATION NOTES	HARVEST DUE/ACTUAL DATE/YIELD

NAME/VARIETY/ SUPPLIER	DATE SOWN & PROPAGATION NOTES

Chromolithograph by G. Severeyns of seven varieties of ornamental gourds, from the *Album Benary* (1876–82) by the Erfurt seedsman Ernst Benary.

CUCURBITS

NAME/VARIETY/ SUPPLIER	DATE SOWN & PROPAGATION NOTES

NAME/VARIETY/ SUPPLIER	DATE SOWN & PROPAGATION NOTES

PLANTING & CULTIVATION NOTES	HARVEST DUE/ACTUAL DATE/YIELD

Chromolithograph by G. Severeyns of eight varieties of tomatoes, from the *Album Benary* (1876–82) by the Erfurt seedsman Ernst Benary.

TOMATOES

NAME/VARIETY/ SUPPLIER	DATE SOWN & PROPAGATION NOTES

NAME/VARIETY/ SUPPLIER	DATE SOWN & PROPAGATION NOTES

Chromolithograph by G. Severeyns of six varieties of sugar, or edible-podded, peas, from the *Album Benary* (1876–82) by the Erfurt seedsman Ernst Benary.

PEAS & BEANS

NAME/VARIETY/ SUPPLIER	DATE SOWN & PROPAGATION NOTES

NAME/VARIETY/ SUPPLIER	DATE SOWN & PROPAGATION NOTES

PLANTING & CULTIVATION NOTES	HARVEST DUE/ACTUAL DATE/YIELD	

Chromolithograph by G. Severeyns of six varieties of cabbages, from the *Album Benary* (1876–82) by the Erfurt seedsman Ernst Benary.

BRASSICAS

NAME/VARIETY/ SUPPLIER	DATE SOWN & PROPAGATION NOTES

NAME/VARIETY/ SUPPLIER	DATE SOWN & PROPAGATION NOTES

PLANTING & CULTIVATION NOTES	HARVEST DUE/ACTUAL DATE/YIELD

Chromolithograph by G. Severeyns of ten varieties of onions, from the *Album Benary* (1876–82) by the Erfurt seedsman Ernst Benary.

ONIONS

NAME/VARIETY/SUPPLIER	DATE SOWN & PROPAGATION NOTES

PLANTING & CULTIVATION NOTES	HARVEST DUE/ACTUAL DATE/YIELD

Chromolithograph by G. Severeyns of thirteen varieties of capsicums or Chili peppers, from the *Album Benary* (1876–82) by the Erfurt seedsman Ernst Benary.

SPECIAL INTEREST

NAME/VARIETY/ SUPPLIER	DATE SOWN & PROPAGATION NOTES

NAME/VARIETY/ SUPPLIER	DATE SOWN & PROPAGATION NOTES

PLANTING & CULTIVATION NOTES	HARVEST DUE/ACTUAL DATE/YIELD

NAME/VARIETY/ SUPPLIER	DATE SOWN & PROPAGATION NOTES

SUPPLIERS

SUPPLIERS

SUPPLIERS